THE WORLD AROUND US

UNDER OUR CLOTHES

Our First Talk About Our Bodies

Dr. Jillian Roberts   Illustrations by Jane Heinrichs

ORCA BOOK PUBLISHERS

I dedicate this book to all the courageous individuals who fight for gender respect and equality. In particular, I am inspired by the social justice warrior Erin Skillen and by all the valiant women and men of the #MeToo movement. Thank you for sharing your powerful voices so that our young people can learn from your strength and truth.
—JR

For my parents, who told me I was beautiful, but, more importantly, told me I was clever, kind and strong when I needed to hear it most.
—JH

Library and Archives Canada Cataloguing in Publication

Title: Under our clothes: our first talk about our bodies / Jillian Roberts ; Jane Heinrichs, illustrator.
Names: Roberts, Jillian, 1971– author. | Heinrichs, Jane, 1982– illustrator.
Series: World around us (Orca Book Publishers); 5.

Description: Series statement: World around us; 5

Identifiers: Canadiana (print) 20190067055 | Canadiana (ebook) 2019006708x | ISBN 9781459820975 (hardcover) | ISBN 9781459820982 (PDF) | ISBN 9781459820999 (EPUB)

Subjects: LCSH: Child sexual abuse—Prevention—Juvenile literature. | LCSH: Child abuse—Prevention—Juvenile literature. | LCSH: Body image—Juvenile literature. | LCSH: Body image in children—Juvenile literature.

Classification: LCC HV6570.R63 2019 | DDC j613.6/6083—dc23

Library of Congress Control Number: 2019934062
Simultaneously published in Canada and the United States in 2019

Summary: In this illustrated nonfiction picture book, child psychologist Dr. Jillian Roberts introduces young readers to the ideas of body safety and body image.

Orca Book Publishers is committed to reducing the consumption of nonrenewable resources in the making of our books. We make every effort to use materials that support a sustainable future.

Orca Book Publishers gratefully acknowledges the support for its publishing programs provided by the following agencies: the Government of Canada, the Canada Council for the Arts and the Province of British Columbia through the BC Arts Council and the Book Publishing Tax Credit.

The author and publisher have made every effort to ensure that the information in this book was correct at the time of publication. The author and publisher do not assume any liability for any loss, damage or disruption caused by errors or omissions. Every effort has been made to trace copyright holders and to obtain their permission for the use of copyrighted material. The publisher apologizes for any errors or omissions and would be grateful if notified of any corrections that should be incorporated in future reprints or editions of this book.

Artwork created using English watercolors and Japanese brush pens on Italian watercolor paper.

Cover and interior art by Jane Heinrichs
Design by Rachel Page

Front cover photos:
Stocksy.com (left), iStock.com (center and right)
Back cover photos:
Stocksy.com (left and center) and iStock.com (right)
Interior photos:
Stocksy.com: © Jamie Grill Atlas p. 11, Erin Drago p. 14, Studio Firma p. 16, Jovo Jovanovic p. 22, Jacques van Zyl p 24, Rob and Julia Campbell p. 25
iStock.com: © DOUGBERRY p. 4, FatCamera p. 5, tzahiV p. 7, kate_sept2004 p. 9, laflor p. 10, Rawpixel p. 17, SolStock p. 19, idildemir p. 20, energyy p. 21, vitapix p 23, AleksandarNakic p. 26, kali9 p. 27, fstop123 p. 28, SolStock p. 29

ORCA BOOK PUBLISHERS
orcabook.com

Printed and bound in China.

22 21 20 19 • 4 3 2 1

O—O—O—O—O—O—O—O—O—O—O—O—O—O—O—O—O—O—O—O—O

When you venture out into the world around us,

you will see people with all kinds of body types. They can be tall, short, thin, round or anything in between. All shapes and sizes of bodies are beautiful. It is important for everyone to feel comfortable in their body, regardless of what size or shape it is. And it is important that everyone respects and takes good care of their body.

O—O—O—O—O—O—O—O—O—O—O—O—O—O—O—O—O—O—O—O—O

When I was in the changeroom last week, I noticed that some people change behind a towel or in private rooms, and others don't mind being seen naked. Why?

Different people have different thoughts and feelings about their bodies. Most of these ideas come from the homes and cultures they were raised in. Some people prefer to behave more modestly—they might want to keep their bodies covered up, even when they are in a changeroom. Other people feel their bodies don't need to be covered, that they are just a part of nature. Different people have different attitudes about their bodies, privacy and modesty, and that's perfectly okay.

What Is Modesty?

To be modest is to act or dress in a way that avoids drawing attention to yourself. Modesty is different for everyone, and it's not just about how you dress but also about how you think and behave. Everyone has different ideas about what modesty means to them, and it is important not to judge others for how they show modesty.

What Is Privacy?

Privacy means being free of unwanted attention. Body privacy means having others respect your personal space and not touching your body or forcing you to show off your body in a way that makes you feel uncomfortable. This means no one should touch you without permission, and no one should ask you to show parts of your body you do not feel comfortable showing.

Privacy also includes your thoughts, values and beliefs. You do not need to share everything that you are thinking or feeling, and you can't expect others to share their private thoughts and feelings with you.

Why are there different change areas for boys and girls?

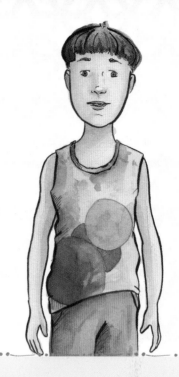

That's a good question! **Many people feel most comfortable changing their clothes only with other people of their same sex—and certain religions and cultures require it.**

The practice of grouping boys and girls separately is common, and in most places around the world you'll see that there are separate public restrooms and changerooms for females and males.

Gender-Neutral Restrooms

A gender-neutral restroom can be used by a person of any gender identity. These bathrooms usually have a sign to show that people of all gender identities are welcome to use the facility. Most bathrooms are divided into male and female spaces. Gender-neutral restrooms are important, as they provide a welcoming and safe space for those who may not fit into the traditional binary system—for instance, those who are transgender or do not identify as either a male or a female. Gender-neutral bathrooms welcome diversity.

If everyone has a body under their clothes, why does it matter? How come we wear bathing suits and have changerooms anyway?

There are parts of our bodies that we consider private, and other parts that we don't. In most cultures, you cover up the parts of your body that are private when you are in public. Your bathing suit and underwear cover your genitals, which are considered your most private parts.

Clothes and bathing suits also help to keep us safe. They remind us which body parts are private and not for others to touch or make us feel uncomfortable about.

And, of course, clothes help to keep us warm!

A Little Bit about Boundaries

Boundaries can be like invisible safety fences around us. One example of a boundary is your "personal bubble." This is the space around your body that belongs to you. When someone makes you uncomfortable by being too close to you, they are crossing a boundary—your personal space boundary. Do you know what your own boundaries are, and what makes you feel uncomfortable? Practice clearly stating your boundaries with an adult you trust. This will help you do it with others as well.

Is it ever okay for someone to look at my private parts?

From time to time a doctor may need to look at or touch the private parts of your body to make sure you are healthy. And when babies and kids are very young, they sometimes need help washing their private parts in the bath. Parents often do this for their children to keep their bodies clean and healthy.

You might see a woman expose her breasts in a public place to feed her baby. This is called breastfeeding. Breastfeeding is a natural thing—moms produce milk in their bodies that contains nutrients to keep their babies nourished and help them grow. And babies don't like waiting for their food, so breastfeeding can happen anywhere and at any time! Some mothers prefer to cover up their breasts and/or nurse in private, and others feed their babies with a bottle. These choices are personal and should be respected.

How do I know when something is right or wrong? I want to keep my body safe, but I'm not sure what to do.

It all starts with knowing what feels comfortable for you and what your boundaries are. The body-safety checklist on this page can help you keep yourself safe and know what to do when something is happening that is not okay.

It's important to know your own boundaries and to respect others' boundaries. We want to feel comfortable, safe and heard and help make our friends and family feel the same way.

Body-Safety Checklist

· **My body belongs to me and no one else:** My body is mine, and only I get to choose how and when it is touched.

· **I know my warning signs:** I know how I feel emotionally and physically when something feels uncomfortable and/or unsafe. I must recognize and respect those feelings.

· **No secrets:** I must always tell a trusted adult if something has happened that has made me feel uncomfortable and/or unsafe. And no one should ever ask me to keep a secret from the trusted adults in my life.

· **Private parts:** I understand which parts of my body are private and off-limits and I understand that these same parts are off-limits on others' bodies. When someone crosses this boundary, or attempts to cross this boundary, I must tell an adult I trust right away.

What if someone touches a different part of my body, one that isn't private, and I don't like it? Can I still say no?

Absolutely. Your body is *your body*, and nobody should be touching any part of it if you don't want them to. And the same goes for you. If somebody tells you not to touch a part of their body, you need to respect them and their personal boundary.

If somebody crosses your personal space boundary, you need to say, "NO!" And if it makes you uncomfortable or has to do with touching your private parts, you need to tell an adult you trust right away. It is never okay for someone to cross your body boundaries or to touch you in a way that makes you feel uncomfortable.

What Is Consent?

Consent is letting people know it's okay to come into your personal bubble. Giving people permission, or consent, is very important because it keeps kids and grown-ups safe. An example of a time when you can give consent is when someone asks for a hug or kiss. It's okay to say no when this happens. You don't have to do things with your body to make other people happy. It's okay to change your mind, to say no sometimes and yes other times depending on how you feel. And it's important for you to ask for consent from others, for you to say, "Do you want a hug?" or "Can I hold your hand?"

When we were little, my sister and I used to take baths together. But now she wants privacy. Did I do something wrong?

It is normal as we get older to feel more modest and to want more privacy. Bodies change as we grow up, and so do our boundaries and our sense of privacy. It doesn't mean you did anything wrong. It means your sister is probably becoming more aware of the private parts of her body, and she is listening to that voice inside her that is saying she needs to ask for more personal space.

As kids grow older and become teens, they begin to experience changes in the body that are part of maturing and becoming adults. This process is called puberty. Puberty can be confusing, and some people feel embarrassed about it, but everyone goes through this period. During puberty both boys and girls begin to produce more hormones in their bodies, but the hormones in boys' bodies act differently than the ones in girls' bodies. Puberty causes changes in height, body shape, where your hair grows, your skin and your emotions and feelings.

My friend always wears a T-shirt at the pool. He says he doesn't like the way he looks. Why would he not like his own body?

It sounds like your friend feels *self-conscious* about his body. This means a person is worried about how they look to others. Your friend might be worried that people will look at him and only see the things he doesn't like about his own body. That might cause him to feel embarrassed.

We should all love the bodies we're in. Unfortunately, people often become self-conscious because we get a lot of messages from the world around us telling us we have to look a certain way. Sometimes when a person doesn't look like people they see in magazines or on TV, they become uncomfortable and feel awkward in their own body.

Body shaming is a type of bullying where people are threatened, insulted or hurt because of their body shape or size. Body shaming can happen when others spread rumors or through online bullying. People who are overweight or underweight or who have something different about their appearance can be targets of body-image bullying.

Our Bodies in the Media

Sometimes young people want to look like the actors and models we see on TV, in magazines and on social media. But actors have help making their hair and makeup look perfect, and the pictures in magazines are often edited and changed. While these are real people, the way they are portrayed to us isn't very realistic, and comparing ourselves to them can just make us feel bad about ourselves. Every person looks, feels and thinks differently, and that is what is most beautiful about all of us.

I wish he didn't worry about that stuff.
I think he's the best!

That's the surprising thing about being self-conscious. The people who know us and love us see the whole person we are, not just what's on the outside.

People tend to think worse of themselves or be harder on themselves than others are on them. This is an important thing to remember—just because you see things about yourself you don't like doesn't mean others see them, and it doesn't mean they agree with how you feel.

I guess sometimes I wish I could change things about the way I look too.

Positive self-talk is a wonderful way to boost your self-esteem and self-confidence! If you start to feel bad about yourself, see if you can change your thinking and build your confidence back up.

Here are some examples of self-talk that will remind you how amazing you are.

- I am thankful for my healthy body. It lets me walk, run, jump and dance!
- I am a really good friend. I care about the people around me.

Just like we have to take care of our bodies, we have to take care of our thoughts, feelings and emotions—our mental health. To take care of our mental health, we can participate in activities that make us feel good, spend time with people we love, and ask for help when we are feeling angry, sad, overwhelmed or any other negative emotion.

Many of us have those thoughts from time to time. But you can work on having *positive self-esteem*, which means being happy with who you are. And the best way to work on building positive self-esteem is to start by accepting yourself and loving yourself just the way you are!

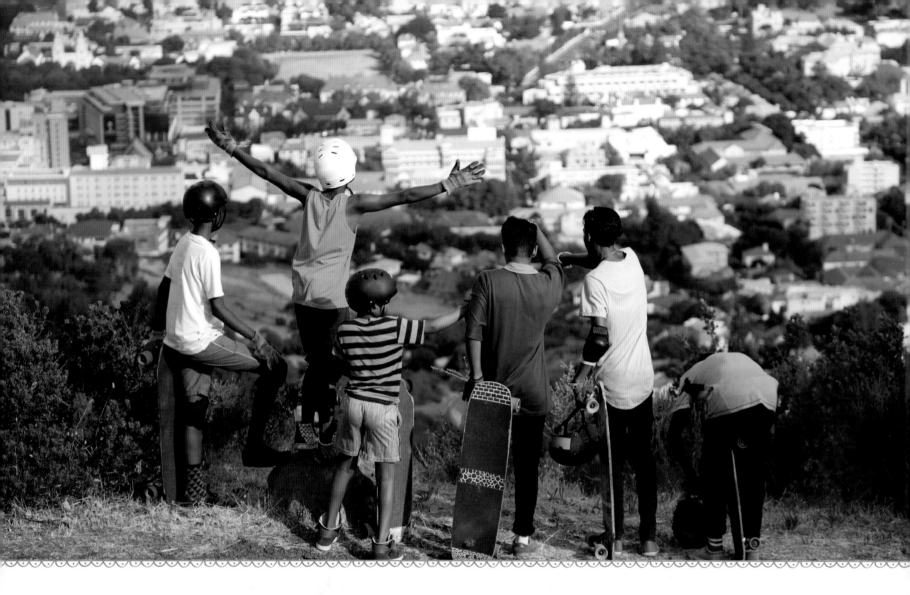

Is there anything I can do to help my friend feel better about himself?

Your friend has to work on his own self-esteem—it comes from within him. But you can help by noticing the things about him that make him so great.

What do you enjoy about your friend?

What are the things about how he lives, acts and behaves that you admire?

What is he good at?

Internal qualities, or character traits, are the ways we act, think or feel. They are not just the ways we act once but the ways we act most of the time. Examples of internal qualities include being kind, being respectful, being honest, being loving and being generous.

Taking the time to appreciate your friends and family for the kind way they act or for their creative ideas can help them build positive self-esteem. And don't forget to acknowledge all the great things about yourself!

Talking about body boundaries and self-esteem is really important. Observing the world around you and learning how different people feel and think will help you build confidence in yourself and help others too. And remember, you can always ask the adults in your life about the things that are on your mind.

A Note from Dr. Jillian Roberts, Author and Child Psychologist

When I was growing up, I didn't feel good about my body. I spent years feeling uncomfortable in my own skin. I didn't learn the lessons I'm trying to share in this book until much later in life. It is one of my greatest hopes that the children of this generation can have a different experience and learn to cherish and take care of their bodies. I've always enjoyed being around people who see beyond what's on the outside. There is so much more to us as people than simply what we look like. I really hope young readers take away from this conversation how special their bodies are and how important it is to learn about body boundaries and build positive self-esteem.

Resources

Online

Anxiety BC: "Helpful Thinking for Younger Children." anxietybc.com/sites/default/files/Healthy_Thinking_for_Younger_Children.pdf

Anxiety BC: "Realistic Thinking." anxietybc.com/sites/default/files/RealisticThinking.pdf

Body Image Health: "The Model for Healthy Body Image and Weight." http://bodyimagehealth.org/model-for-healthy-body-image/

Eating Disorder Hope: "Bullying and Body Image." eatingdisorderhope.com/information/eating-disorder/bullying-and-body-image

Girls' Respect Groups: "Self-Respect for Children: What Is It?" girlsrespectgroups.com/self-respect-for-children-what-is-it/

I Respect Myself: "What Is Puberty?" irespectmyself.ca/en/respect-yourself/healthy-body/puberty/what-is-puberty

Kidz Search: "Modesty" wiki. kidzsearch.com/wiki/Modesty

Media Smarts: "Talking to Kids About Media and Body Image" tip sheet. mediasmarts.ca/teacher-resources/talking-kids-about-media-body-image-tip-sheet

Study.com: "Body Language: Lesson for Kids." study.com/academy/lesson/body-language-lesson-for-kids.html

Super Duper Publications: "Personal Space—A Social Skill." superduperinc.com/handouts/pdf/239_Personal_Space.pdf

Talking With Trees: "What Is Character?" talkingtreebooks.com/definition/what-is-character-definition.html

The Virtues Project: "Defining the Virtues." virtuesproject.com/virtuesdef.html#

Women's and Children's Health Network: "Self-Esteem—Feeling Good about Yourself." cyh.com/HealthTopics/HealthTopicDetailsKids.aspx?p=335&np=287&id=1588

Women's and Children's Health Network: "What Is Puberty?" cyh.com/HealthTopics/HealthTopicDetailsKids.aspx?p=335&np=289&id=1828

Print

Byers, Grace. *I Am Enough*. New York, NY: Balzer + Bray, 2018.

Howe, James. *Brontorina*. Somerville, MA: Candlewick Press, 2013.

King, Kimberly and Zack. *I Said No!: A Kid-To-Kid Guide to Keeping Your Private Parts Private*. Weaverville, CA: Boulden Pub, 2008.

Roberts, Jillian. *Where Do Babies Come From?: Our First Talk About Birth*. Victoria, BC: Orca Book Publishers, 2015.

Starishevsky, Jill. *My Body Belongs to Me*. New York, NY: Safety Star Media, 2009.

THE WORLD AROUND US series

ON OUR STREET
Our First Talk About Poverty

Dr. Jillian Roberts and Jaime Casap Illustrations by Jane Heinrichs

9781459816176 · $19.95 HC

ON THE NEWS
Our First Talk About Tragedy

Dr. Jillian Roberts Illustrations by Jane Heinrichs

9781459817845 · $19.95 HC

ON THE PLAYGROUND
Our First Talk About Prejudice

Dr. Jillian Roberts Illustrations by Jane Heinrichs

9781459820913 · $19.95 HC

ON THE INTERNET
Our First Talk About Online Safety

Dr. Jillian Roberts Illustrations by Jane Heinrichs

9781459820944 · $19.95 HC

These inquiry-based books are an excellent cross-curricular resource encouraging children to explore and discuss important issues and **foster their own compassion and empathy.**

AGES 6–8 · 32 PAGES
FULL-COLOR PHOTOGRAPHS · RESOURCES INCLUDED

TheWorldAroundUsSeries.com